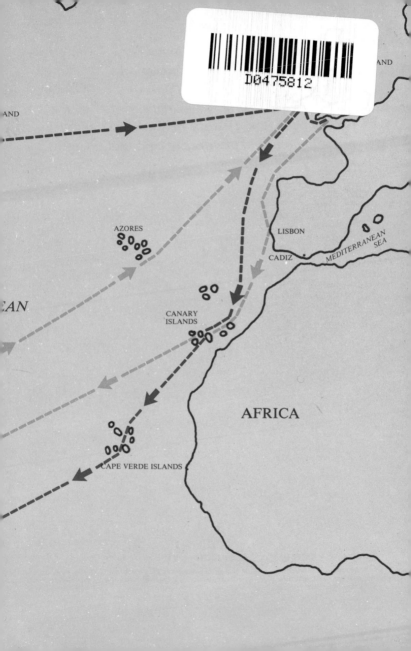

Elizabeth the First surrounded herself with great men, and one of her favourites was Sir Walter Raleigh. Good looking, gallant, and both adventurous and scholarly, he is remembered as much for his book The History of the World *as for his brave fighting and his ideas of colonisation. Here is his story.*

Sir Walter Raleigh

written and illustrated
by FRANK HUMPHRIS

Ladybird Books Loughborough

The boyhood of Raleigh was spent at a time when England was emerging from the trials and religious persecutions of the previous reign, into one of the most notable periods in our history.

Queen Elizabeth the First was on the throne, and during her reign the country produced a number of remarkable men whose ability, courage and daring made England mistress of the seas.

Among these was Walter Raleigh. He was about six years old when the young queen came to the throne in 1558, and like so many of the great sailors of his day he was born in Devon, the son of a country gentleman. From his earliest years he showed an aptitude both for learning and adventure.

Cousins, uncles, and even Raleigh's half-brother — they were all famous seamen who could tell exciting stories of adventure and exploration

He grew up with much to inspire him, for he was related to several of the most famous sea captains of the day. His uncle was Sir Henry Champernoun, Vice Admiral of the West; his elder half-brother was Humphrey, later Sir Humphrey Gilbert the noted navigator and explorer; Sir Richard Grenville and Sir Francis Drake were cousins.

As a boy, he must have heard many tales of exploration and adventure. He must have listened eagerly to stories of the long voyages over the western ocean to the Americas, of the Spanish galleons sailing home with their holds full of treasure in silver and gold, and of new sea routes to the east and unknown lands waiting to be discovered.

Like most young boys living near the sea Raleigh would have learned to sail and handle a boat under all sorts of conditions. In those days there were none of the modern aids to navigation, and men had to learn every trick of the tide and the weather by experience. Also, the boats were awkward and clumsy by comparison with the sleek, well designed yachts of today.

For young Raleigh it was wonderful training for the long and dangerous voyages that lay ahead. Voyages that were to lead to the very beginnings of English settlement overseas and to the start of the British Empire.

Raleigh learned to sail in a small boat

Walter Raleigh was probably in his teens when he became a student at Oriel College, Oxford. (Undergraduates at that time could be as young as ten years old, or as old as twenty five.) Although Raleigh enjoyed his studies, he left without a degree

However, life was not all playing around by the sea and sailing small boats. There were lessons, for education was most important for a boy of good family to enable him to take his proper place in the world. Raleigh was a keen pupil, eager to learn and absorb new facts. Sometime in his teens he left Devon and went to Oxford, where he was soon known as an outstanding character among the junior members.

Here he found another great interest in the world of books, second only to his love of adventure and the sea. Walter Raleigh was to become one of the noted scholars of the age. He wrote poetry as well as prose, and later in life he began to write a history of the world.

After only a short period at Oxford and before he was seventeen, he sought adventure and excitement by joining a band of English soldiers who had volunteered to fight in the religious wars of France.

At that time Europe was deeply divided into those who adopted the new Protestant cause and those who followed the old Catholic faith. Unfortunately, this new religious movement, known as the *Reformation*, brought not peace but war to the nations north of the Alps. France, Holland and Germany were the countries most affected and the struggles were long and incredibly bitter.

In France, the Catholics led by the King were mostly the victors and the Protestants, or Huguenots as they were called, were ruthlessly persecuted.

The battle of Jarnac

However, several of the noblest and most powerful families in the land supported the Protestant cause and from time to time they had successes under the leadership of the great Admiral Coligny, Prince Condé, and the Queen of Navarre.

Then in 1569 disaster overtook the Huguenots at the battle of Jarnac where they were thoroughly defeated and Prince Condé was killed. It is believed Walter Raleigh took part in this battle. He and the other English soldiers, being Protestants, fought on the side of the Huguenots and only after severe fighting did they manage to force their way through the ranks of the enemy.

Raleigh spent some five or six years as a soldier on the continent before returning to England.

By the spring of 1575 Raleigh was back in London as a member of the Middle Temple but without studying law. He seems to have been simply enjoying life, and he got into a few escapades with his boisterous companions. On one occasion he was jailed for a week for fighting with the son of Sir John Perrot.

One of his great friends was George Gascoigne, ex-soldier, adventurer, Cambridge scholar, Member of Parliament for Bedfordshire and a brilliant writer, important for some of the new forms of literature that he introduced.

Raleigh too was a budding young poet and writer, and the first example of his printed verse dates from this time. But the tall, black-browed young man was as impetuous and outspoken in his writing as in his speech. It was a characteristic that was to make him many enemies in the future.

With no soldiering and no occupation other than writing, the two men, Raleigh and Gascoigne, together with the sea captain, Martin Frobisher, used to gather at Sir Humphrey Gilbert's house overlooking the docks. There they would watch the shipping in the busy river, and spend hours discussing the design and rigging of ships and the future voyages they hoped to make.

Voyages of adventure and discovery in as yet unexplored lands, to bring them all riches and fame.

Raleigh and his friends used to meet at Sir Humphrey Gilbert's house

Raleigh made his first voyage to the west in the year 1578, as joint leader of an expedition organised by his half-brother, Sir Humphrey Gilbert. Gilbert, some fourteen years older than Raleigh, had obtained official permission to discover 'any remote and barbarous lands' and claim them for the crown. The idea also was to sail to the northern coasts of north America to see if there was a sea passage round the top of the continent – a North-West passage – through the Arctic Ocean south to India and Cathay, as China was then called.

Raleigh commanded the *Falcon*, a ship of one hundred tons, incredibly small by modern standards for such a voyage.

The expedition seemed doomed from the start. The fleet of seven ships had reached the Azores, a group of islands in mid Atlantic roughly on a level with Spain, when strong gales drove it back to port. Here the damaged ships were repaired and set out again into the even worse storms of winter. Then Gilbert quarrelled with one of his captains, Knollys, who finally deserted and sailed back to England.

Spain had little doubt that the main purpose of the expedition was to attack her ships or possessions overseas, and the Spanish fleet had been warned to be on the look-out. A fierce but indecisive fight took place off Cape Verde where Raleigh lost many men and was nearly killed himself. In 1579 the battered fleet returned. Raleigh had gained experience – if little else.

Raleigh made his first voyage of exploration as joint leader (with Sir Humphrey Gilbert) of the expedition

Their sea venture having failed, both Gilbert and Raleigh now turned soldiers. The Irish were in a state of rebellion, encouraged and helped by Spain and the continental powers with whom England was officially at peace.

Raleigh was made a captain in charge of a company of one hundred men, and he tackled the difficult task with his usual force. This was very different from anything which he had known before. It was a wild country and the conditions were appalling. At night the rebels would swarm out of hiding and attack the villages, killing and setting fire to the huts before vanishing again into the woods and treacherous Irish bogs. Nowadays, we would call this guerilla warfare.

Raleigh leading his men against the Irish rebels

In Raleigh's own words it was to 'fight as one beating the air.'

There were quarrels too among the English commanders. Raleigh, fiercely loyal to his brother and hero, Sir Humphrey Gilbert, was outspoken in his criticism of the Lord Deputy of Ireland and the Commander in Chief.

None the less his name became a byword for ruthless and dare-devil courage. On one occasion, he held a ford single-handed while his men escaped across the river. On another, he rushed back into a horde of enemies to rescue a friend, and once he captured an Irish chieftain in his own stronghold and brought him back a prisoner.

In December 1581 Raleigh was sent back to England with dispatches from the Governor of Munster, one of the Irish provinces. Coming to the court (which was then at Greenwich), he attracted the attention of the Queen. This may have been because of his outspoken criticism of the position in Ireland in front of the council, or it may simply have been his undoubted good looks and striking appearance, and his bold and dashing reputation. The Queen loved to be surrounded by handsome young men.

The much quoted incident of the cloak may be equally true or untrue. It was quite in keeping with Walter Raleigh's character.

The story goes that one day Elizabeth was walking in the grounds surrounded by her courtiers. Suddenly she stopped. There was a wet and muddy area on the path in front of her. As the courtiers hesitated, not knowing quite what to do, Raleigh stepped forward and, taking off his fine velvet cloak, spread it across the mud at the Queen's feet.

It was a typically flamboyant gesture and one that would certainly have attracted Elizabeth's attention. The Queen was unlikely to overlook a young man who was willing to sacrifice a valuable cloak so that she should not get her feet wet, and Raleigh rose rapidly in the royal favour. From a gentleman soldier of fortune, he became a privileged courtier.

At that period in our history, it was the custom for the sovereign to reward men of distinction with gifts of land and property, and also with grants which gave them control of certain licences.

The Queen gave Raleigh the licence to export woollen cloth, then one of our most important articles of trade. This meant that he was paid a tax for every yard of cloth that was sold. Later he was given the monopoly of wine licences, and Raleigh was soon a very rich man.

He was also given large estates and a fine house in the Strand where he could entertain distinguished guests in a style suitable to his position as one of the great men at court. Durham House, as it was called, was situated on the banks of the Thames. From Raleigh's study, which was in a turret overlooking the river, he could watch the ships sailing down towards the sea.

He was noted for the magnificence of his appearance. Large sums were spent in buying armour and fine clothes, jewels, books and pictures.

Strangely enough, he never lost his broad but pleasant Devonshire accent. This may have added to his charm, for he was a witty and entertaining speaker. However, he was not popular with everyone. His rapid rise to fame and fortune created jealousy and dislike among certain of the courtiers.

Trading licences for wool and wine
made Walter Raleigh very rich

As Raleigh grew in favour with the Queen he was granted further honours. In 1584 Elizabeth made him a knight. He was now Sir Walter Raleigh, one of the wealthiest and most powerful men in the kingdom.

He led a very busy and active life. One of his commissions was to direct enquiries into the Navy, a task for which he was well suited and he was also given a commission to clear the seas of Portuguese privateers. Unlike pirates, who attacked any ship and were outlawed by their own country, privateers were vessels owned by a private person, or company, with government authority to attack and plunder ships belonging to an enemy.

The word 'enemy' was often very loosely defined and any ships other than those belonging to their own country were liable to be attacked. At one time or another most of the English seamen were privateers. Sir Francis Drake was one of the most famous and Hawkins, Frobisher and others were noted for their privateering activities.

Raleigh did not personally lead an expedition against the Portuguese marauders, but he could issue authority to English ships to seek them out and attack them wherever they were found.

The highest honour of all that he received, however, was to be made Captain of the Yeomen of the Guard. This meant protecting the Queen's person at all times, an important position which brought him into daily contact with the Queen.

Queen Elizabeth knights Walter Raleigh

Honours continued to shower upon Raleigh. He was made Lord Lieutenant of the County of Cornwall and Vice-Admiral of Devon and Cornwall. Another of his appointments was as Warden of the Stannaries, a post which put him in control of the tin mines in Devon and Cornwall. Raleigh, being a Devon man himself, had considerable sympathy and understanding of the conditions and problems of the miners, and he was responsible for several reforms.

For the most part, the tin miners made their own laws and held their courts in a chosen area on Crockern Tor in the middle of Dartmoor, where there was an ancient stone table and seats. Here, as Lord

Sir Walter Raleigh rides to meet the tin-miners

Warden, Raleigh would sit with his 'stannators' and listen to the arguments and grievances of the tin miners. They liked and trusted him to work on their behalf.

Like many a great landowner and important man, Raleigh entered Parliament and became the member for his county, Devonshire. In those days it was the duty of such men to go into Parliament. This was long before ordinary people had the vote and could choose whom they wished to represent them as Members. The House of Commons did not have anything like as much power then as it has now. If the Queen did not agree with anything the Members did, she simply over-ruled them.

All this time the thoughts of exploration and colonisation were never far from Raleigh's mind. Many schemes had been discussed with his half-brother, Sir Humphrey Gilbert. Gilbert himself had spent most of his own fortune and that of his wife's in various endeavours, but still he was determined to plant a colony of Englishmen on the shores of North America.

He had got his 'Letters Patent' to discover and occupy lands not possessed by any other Christian power, the lands to belong to Gilbert and his heirs under the Crown.

In 1583, when Raleigh was first establishing himself at court, Gilbert got together a fleet of five small ships, the largest of which was outfitted by Raleigh. The Queen however prevented Raleigh from joining the expedition. The fleet sailed and eventually reached the fine harbour of what is now St John's in

Newfoundland, which Gilbert took possession of in the name of the Queen. So Newfoundland became our first and oldest colony.

Leaving the shores of Newfoundland, Gilbert started to sail south along the little known mainland coast of North America. Then one of the ships ran aground and was lost with most of the stores and equipment necessary for founding a colony. There was nothing for it but to return, and on the homeward voyage Gilbert himself was drowned when his ship sank.

Sir Humphrey Gilbert's expedition sails for Newfoundland

25

Following, the death of Sir Humphrey Gilbert, Raleigh obtained a new charter for exploration. In 1584 he sent out a preliminary expedition of two ships to America. These were to explore the possibilities of founding an English colony between the northern area around Newfoundland and the Spanish possessions in central America.

Instead of sailing first to Newfoundland, as Gilbert had done, they sailed by way of Florida and landed on the coast of what is now North Carolina.

When the two captains returned from their voyage they reported very favourably on the rich land they had found: "the soil is the most plentiful, sweet, fruitful and wholesome in all the world ... the people most gentle, loving and faithful, void of all guile and treason, and such as live after the manner of the golden age." It seemed that they had discovered an earthly paradise.

Raleigh and his friends were inspired by this report and decided that here was an ideal place to start a colony. In the spring of the following year – 1585 – the expedition set sail, commanded by Sir Richard Grenville, Raleigh's cousin. Raleigh desperately wanted to lead it himself but again he was prevented by the Queen who required his presence at court.

Four months after leaving England they landed on what is now Roanoke Island in Pimlico Sound. They named the land Virginia, to honour the Queen.

The new settlement is named Virginia, in honour of the Queen

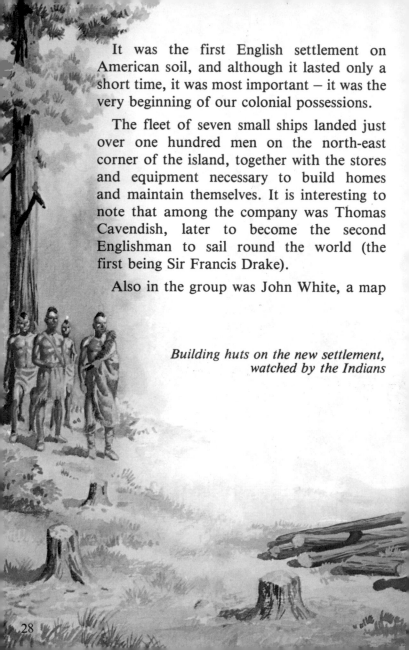

It was the first English settlement on American soil, and although it lasted only a short time, it was most important — it was the very beginning of our colonial possessions.

The fleet of seven small ships landed just over one hundred men on the north-east corner of the island, together with the stores and equipment necessary to build homes and maintain themselves. It is interesting to note that among the company was Thomas Cavendish, later to become the second Englishman to sail round the world (the first being Sir Francis Drake).

Also in the group was John White, a map

Building huts on the new settlement, watched by the Indians

maker and artist, who made several water-colour sketches of the natives and their villages.

Soon the men were hard at work marking out the site of the settlement and chopping down trees to build their huts. Then land had to be cleared for the planting of crops, for the colonists had to become self-supporting as soon as possible, as the stores brought by the ships were limited.

It was not long before the settlement was visited by the native Indians, who showed great curiosity at seeing the colonists working with saw and axe. They themselves had only stone and flint tools.

At first the Indians welcomed the English and proved friendly and helpful. The colonists were glad of this help, since they lacked experience of the country and many of the plants were new to them. They were also on their own now because the ships had returned to England.

Unfortunately, as time went on things began to go wrong with the little colony on Roanoke Island. The crops they had planted failed. They may have been using the wrong sort of seed, or the soil may have been unsuitable for cultivation with the primitive methods they had.

This was a serious matter, for the failure of the crops meant that there was no corn to make bread. The colonists faced a hungry winter, for there was just not enough food in the area to support both the Indians and the Europeans.

Other serious problems arose. As the once friendly Indians realised that the white man had come to take away their land, their friendliness turned to anger and suspicion.

At last there was open conflict, in which some of the Indians were killed. Now the English had the added problem of being on constant guard, and as yet there was no sign of Grenville, who was expected to return with further supplies. When Sir Francis Drake's ships, homeward bound from the West Indies, anchored off the island, the desperate colonists abandoned the settlement and returned home.

The Indians grew angry with the settlers

Two weeks later, Grenville arrived at Roanoke and found the settlement deserted. He searched the surrounding country, then returned to England. This failure was a bitter disappointment for both Raleigh and Grenville. Nonetheless, Raleigh persevered with his idea of founding a colony in Virginia.

In 1587 a new expedition was organised consisting of over a hundred men and women, with John White as governor. As already mentioned John White was an artist, and fortunately some of his sketches have survived. They show Indian life at that period.

It seemed at first as if this enterprise might have a better chance of survival, but events proved other-

Part of the Indian village of Secoton, showing huts made of bark and neat fields of corn (after John White's painting)

Indians fishing in the shallow water round Roanoke Island (after John White's painting)

wise. The Indians had not forgotten the previous colony, and there was disagreement and lack of discipline among the colonists.

John White returned to England to organise further supplies. He brought news that the settlers were landed safely at Roanoke and that a baby girl had been born and named Virginia Dare, the first English child born in America.

That was the last that was ever heard of the colony. It was now 1588, the year of the Armada, so the supply ships were unable to sail as all ships were needed for England's defence. It was two years before any ships reached Roanoke again, and by then the colony had utterly disappeared.

Raleigh made no further attempt to colonise Virginia. He had spent many years and a vast fortune on the various expeditions, but now he made his charter over to Richard Hakluyt, the historian.

There were some lasting results from these early voyages however. One was the introduction of potatoes, the roots of which had been brought back from Virginia. Raleigh was enthusiastic, and experimented by planting them on his vast estates in Ireland.

He is also credited with introducing tobacco and the habit of smoking to England. The habit spread with amazing rapidity, particularly among the English upper classes. There is an amusing story that when a servant came into the room one day and saw Raleigh smoking for the first time, he thought he was on fire and threw a jug of ale over him.

While Raleigh was busy with his colonising efforts, events had reached a climax with Spain. The fragile, so-called peace was at an end. The Spanish king, Philip II, had decided that the time was ripe for the invasion and overthrow of England which he had long been planning.

The overall strategy was for a huge fleet to transport thousands of troops from Spain to link up with the Spanish army already in the Netherlands. The combined force would then cross the Channel and invade England.

Putting the fire out!

A great Armada was assembled in the various Spanish ports with the main concentration at Cadiz. By 1587, preparations were well advanced when Sir Francis Drake carried out his famous and daring raid on Cadiz, destroying thirty three ships and a vast quantity of stores. This delayed the action for a year.

The Armada finally put to sea in 1588, and on the 19th July the huge fleet was sighted sailing up the English Channel. The Spanish were confident of their overwhelming strength, but · the smaller, faster English vessels kept pounding them with their long-range cannon, then veering out of range.

The running fight continued up the Channel until the Spanish fleet anchored off Calais, where they

Fighting the Spanish Armada

were to link up with the army of the Duke of Parma.

How the English fire-ships scattered the great fleet, and how, the following day, the fighting continued until the Spanish galleons were driven into the North Sea, can be read in the Ladybird book, *Sir Francis Drake*.

Walter Raleigh was not given a command at sea during the early stages of the battle. His duties lay in organising the defences of the west country, where the local militia and all able bodied men were mobilised in readiness, should the Spanish attempt a landing there. Once it was known that the Armada was making for Calais, Raleigh hurried back to London and joined the English fleet for the final battle.

The years following the Armada were full of activity and adventure for Raleigh. At court, the Queen now had a new favourite, the young Earl of Essex. Although Raleigh was still held in great esteem, there was constant rivalry between the two.

During this period he took the opportunity to visit his vast estates in Ireland.

With his cousin, Sir Francis Drake, he also took part in an expedition of reprisals for the Armada. The campaign against the Portuguese ports was costly, but some two hundred enemy ships were destroyed.

In 1591 he was appointed second-in-command of a squadron of six ships to intercept the Spanish treasure fleet, but Elizabeth refused to let him go. His place was taken by his cousin, Sir Richard Grenville.

The last fight of the *Revenge* is one of the most famous in history. Over twenty large Spanish galleons escorted the treasure ships and Grenville, instead of escaping with the other English ships, arrogantly decided to cut his way through the enemy fleet alone. The fighting went on for several hours, with the *Revenge* surrounded by Spanish ships.

Two of the galleons were sunk and tremendous damage done before the *Revenge* at last had to surrender. Grenville died soon after the battle, and a few days later the *Revenge* and many Spanish vessels sank in a violent storm.

The last fight of the Revenge

In the following year, 1592, Raleigh outfitted a stronger squadron which succeeded in capturing the great carrack, *Madre de Dios*, with treasure valued at half a million pounds.

Raleigh had accompanied the expedition as far as Cape Finisterre but on his arrival home he found himself in disgrace. The Queen had discovered his secret marriage to one of her Maids of Honour, Elizabeth Throckmorton. She was furious with his deception, and had him put in the Tower.

He was there for some months, but upon his release, being free from the restrictions of court life, he was able once again to think of overseas exploration. He obtained the Queen's permission to go, and no doubt hoped that a successful venture would

restore him to the royal favour.

This time the objective was Guiana in South America, where wonderfully rich gold mines were supposed to exist, and even an 'El Dorado' – a city of gold. This fabulous land was supposed to be far inland. Raleigh reached the Spanish-held island of Trinidad, which he attacked, then made for the mouth of the River Orinoco on the mainland. He travelled far up the great river until flood water brought the boats to a halt.

Of course no golden city was ever found, only dense jungle, and the expedition returned. Raleigh however was convinced of the wealth to be discovered, and he determined to try again at a later date.

Raleigh and his men on the Orinoco River

At sea there was continuous activity and conflict between England and Spain. There was also renewed danger from another direction. A formal alliance between the King of Spain and one of the Irish leaders gave rise to fears of an invasion by Spain, using Ireland as a base.

The old sea-dogs, Hawkins, Drake and Frobisher were now dead, and Raleigh was called upon to collaborate with Essex for the protection of England's coasts against the fast recovering power of Spain. A strong fleet was gathered together and divided into four squadrons, one of them under Raleigh.

On the morning of June 20th 1596 the fleet approached the Spanish naval base of Cadiz. Raleigh himself had taken his squadron along the coast to intercept any enemy ship likely to give warning to the town, but in the meantime the attack had begun badly.

Instead of dealing with the galleons drawn up in the harbour, it had been decided to attack the town first, in spite of the heavy seas running which capsized several of the boats. When Raleigh returned he realised that everything favoured an attack on the galleons, and worked hard to persuade the other commanders to alter their tactics. He himself, in his ship the *Warspite*, led the attack.

The firing was intense, but the attack was pressed home. Of the four great galleons moored across the narrowest part of the channel, two were burnt and sunk and two captured.

Raleigh leads the attack against the galleons

There was no further resistance from the Spanish ships and the town lay open to attack. The Spaniards seemed shattered by the blow.

Thousands took refuge in the churches, many hiding their valuables among the tombs – and thus saved them, for the English generously agreed not to search the churches. The rest of the town was given over to spoil.

There was also massive destruction among the shipping in the harbour. As well as the four great galleons captured or sunk, seventeen other ships and cargoes worth an estimated twelve millions were lost.

The town of Cadiz under attack

Raleigh however knew little of this. During the fighting at the harbour he had been badly wounded, a wound which caused a limp for the rest of his life.

It is ironic that the man who had done more than any of the other leaders to make victory possible should profit so little.

For it was Essex, officially in command of the land forces, who received huge ransoms for the important prisoners. Essex became the popular hero of the campaign, but there is no question that the real victor of Cadiz was Sir Walter Raleigh.

Seven years after the successful attack on Cadiz, the long reign of Elizabeth came to an end in 1603. With the death of the Queen, Raleigh lost a friend and gained an enemy. The new king, James I, hated him from the beginning.

James was the son of the unfortunate Mary, Queen of Scots, a crafty, suspicious and craven man who was at the same time, something of a scholar. Many of the courtiers, eager to curry favour with the new king, were quick to poison his mind against Raleigh.

Raleigh, as outspoken and independent as ever, had not gone out of his way to please the new monarch. James was only too ready to believe what he was told and consider Raleigh as an enemy. Raleigh, conscious that he had done no wrong, failed to see the danger.

One by one his official posts and privileges were taken from him. Finally he was brought to trial on a trumped-up charge of conspiracy, and sent to the Tower. He was there for thirteen years, in spite of all efforts to obtain his release, but he made splendid use of his time.

He wrote books on several subjects and made experiments in chemistry, but above all he completed the first volume of a *History of the World*, which won praise from everyone except the mean-spirited James.

Raleigh working while in the Tower of London

At length, in 1616, James released him on condition that he led an expedition to Guiana to search for the untold wealth that was supposed to be there. Raleigh himself had promised to bring back a shipload of gold for the king's treasury. He was commanded not to cause damage to any Spanish property or to attack any Spaniard, for James was anxious to remain at peace with Spain. These commands Raleigh promised to obey.

On arrival at Guiana he was very ill with fever and quite unable to undertake the arduous and difficult journey up the Orinoco. The men, who included Raleigh's son, were put in the charge of Lawrence Keymis, one of Raleigh's old comrades. What neither commander knew was that the Spanish had fortified one of the small towns on the route, and as the English passed they were fired upon.

Keymis made no attempt to return the fire, but at about one o'clock the following night, the Spaniards made a surprise attack on the English camp. In the furious fight that followed Raleigh's son was killed, and his comrades avenged his death by storming and taking the town.

With no hope of continuing the search for gold, the expedition struggled back to the coast. Heart-broken at the death of his son, and faced with near mutiny among the men, Raleigh had no alternative but to make his way back to England.

A surprise attack by the Spanish

In doing so Raleigh knew that he faced the wrath of King James, for the whole expedition had been a disastrous failure. Not only had no gold been discovered but fighting had occurred and a Spanish town had been captured and sacked. The Spanish ambassador denounced Raleigh as a pirate and demanded his death for the damage done to Spanish possessions.

Raleigh was again confined to the Tower while an enquiry was held, but even James could not prove that Raleigh had wilfully disobeyed his commands. Nevertheless, he was determined to have Raleigh put to death and ordered that he should be executed on the old charge of conspiracy on which he had been sentenced fifteen years before.

The sentence was carried out on a cold October day, 1618, and Walter Raleigh died, bravely, as he had lived.

Raleigh holds a unique place in our history. He was among the first to see the possibilities of a new England overseas. Although in his lifetime his own attempts at founding colonies in America were not successful, the ideas were implanted in other men's minds. Within a few years of his death, the first permanent settlement was established in America.

In an age of great men – sailors, soldiers, explorers, scholars and poets – Walter Raleigh stands out amongst the greatest.

He was the last of the gallant Elizabethans.

Sir Walter Raleigh walks bravely to his death

INDEX